Sunny Cave

The Mill of Monet

Rives of Light

Mulberry Bridge

For Sale

Pachyderm Forest

Cobblestone Path

Ramshorn Orchard

Village of Tree Gnomes

Unicorn Canyon

Sun Day, the Not-Quite Knight

written by Daniel T. Marsano
drawings by J.H. Stroschin

For my son, Joe,
Who, much like "Sun Day,"
Continues to question,
In quite the same way.

For all that you are,
And all that you've been,
I love you, Joe,
My son, and my friend.

D.T.M.

ISBN 1 - 883960 - 13 - 4

Henry Quill Press
J.H. Stroschin
7340 Lake Drive
Fremont, Michigan 49412-9146

Legends, they say,
Are born in the mind,
And the truth in some cases,
Is quite hard to find.

So judge for yourself,
And examine each rhyme,
As this story begins;
Once upon a time -

In a beautiful kingdom,
In a land far away,
Stood a vine covered castle,
That was home to Sir Day.

And the great knight had married,
The love of his life,
So the Princess To-Day,
Was his lovely young wife.

About a year later,
And to their great joy,
This quite happy couple,
Gave birth to a boy.

But they could not decide,
What to name the young lad,
What best would befit,
This child that they had.

So as time passed on by,
And he still had no name,
They just called the boy, "Son,"
And he came - just the same.

This left but one question,
For Sir Day and his bride,
How to spell the boy's name?
This, they'd have to decide.

Then they thought of the symbol,
Sir Day wore on his chest,
And they knew right away,
That S - U - N was the best.

Now also residing,
In this castle keep,
Down, deep in the cellar,
Reading books or asleep;

There dwelt a winged creature,
With green scales and black eyes,
A fire breathing dragon,
But in three foot tall size.

Though quite small in stature,
Yester had a huge heart,
And as Castle Librarian,
He was remarkably smart.

So it was no surprise,
That Sun liked to spend
The bulk of his free time,
With his sleepy, old friend.

Now Yester taught Sun,
To imagine and dream,
To think and to question,
If things are as they seem.

"Ask Why?" said the dragon,
"Who?, What?, When? and Where?:"
"Ask How?" he continued,
"Life's answers are there!"

Sun did not always know
What Yester's words meant,
But still he enjoyed,
All the time that they spent;

Usually reading,
For as Yester would say,
They must continue to learn,
Something new, EVERY Day.

But when Sun turned sixteen,
He was ready to go,
For he thought that he knew
All he needed to know.

This boy was no different,
Than others, you see,
We all think we're grown up,
Before we're ready to be.

So it was with young Sun,
But in this special land,
A boy had to prove worthy
Of being a man.

He must study and train,
And learn how to fight,
Then face a great challenge,
Before becoming a knight.

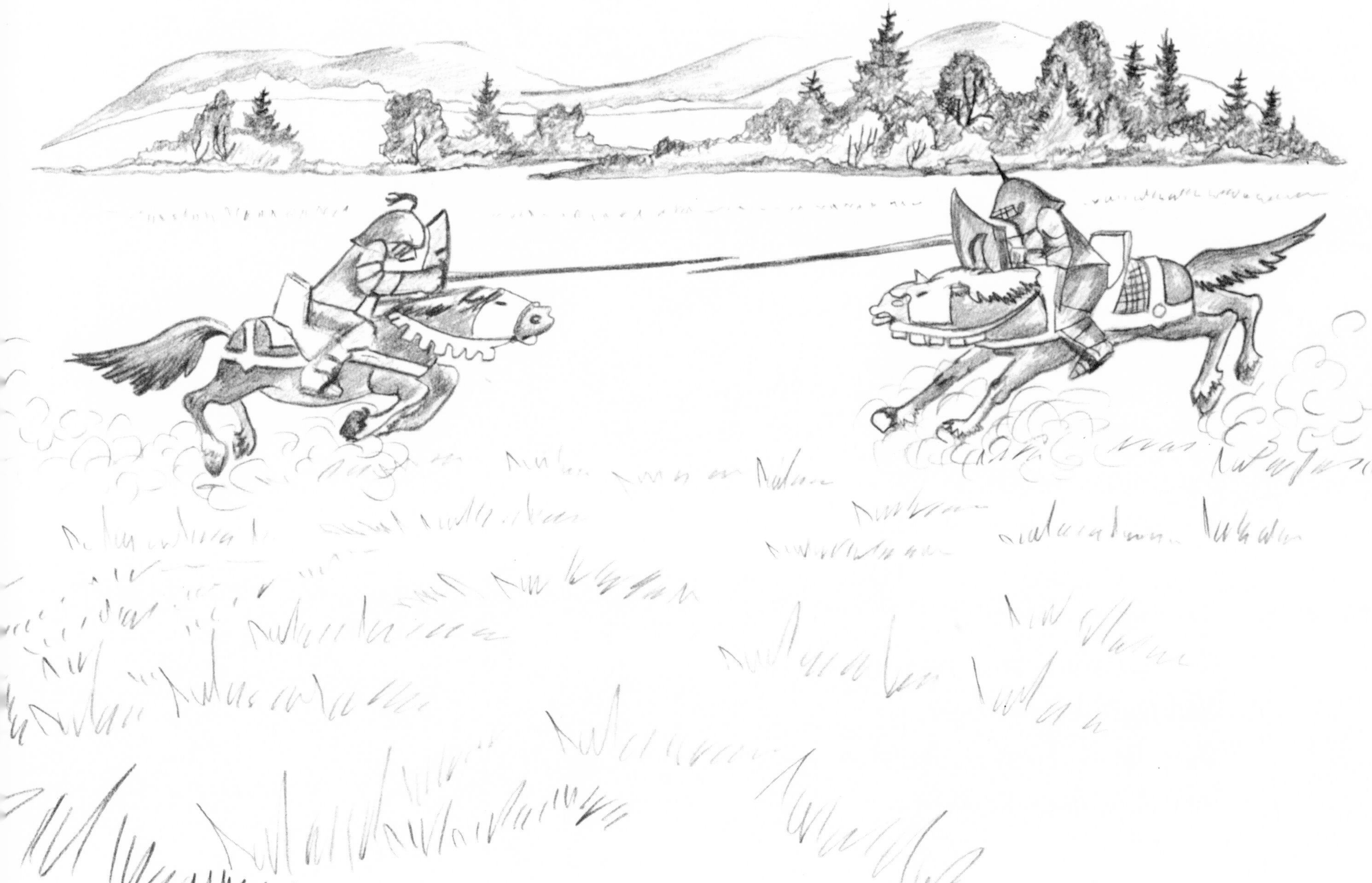

And a knight he must be,
Like all other young men,
That's the way that it was,
As it always had been.

So Sun asked his father,
To go see the King,
He said he was now ready,
"To do this knight thing!"

"I can do this," he said,
"It can't be too tough!
Prance around on a horse,
And do all that knight stuff!"

"I can learn how to smite,
And to handle a lance,
Just don't expect me to wear,
Those aluminum pants!"

So off they both went,
To meet with King Week,
Who thought long and hard,
Before beginning to speak.

"As you know," the King said,
"I can't grant what you ask,
Before becoming a knight,
You must complete a great task."

"You must meet a challenge,
From beginning to end;
That's the way that it is,
As it always has been."

"The challenge, this Day,
Is to go to the East,
Cross the Mulberry Bridge,
And defeat the Troll Beast."

"It sits on that bridge,
With its eyes black as coal,
And those who cross there,
Have to pay the Bridge Troll!"

"It's a large, ugly creature,
That stands ten feet high,
Slay that thing!" said the King,
To which Sun replied, ------ "WHY?"

Now this was a question,
King Week had not heard,
One who speaks to a King,
Does not use the "Why?" word.

"Why, indeed!" said the King,
"You want to know why?
Do you now believe,
You are wiser than I?"

"Just because," he went on,
"That's the way that it is.

That big ugly Troll,
Thinks that whole bridge is his!"

"WHO says that it's not?"
Sun wanted to know,
"WHAT proof do we have?
WHERE does it say so?"

"WHEN was it built?
And HOW and by whom?
These are things we should ask,
It's not fair to assume!"

"Questions," the King said,
"You ask me so many,
When no one before you,
Has dared to ask any."

"Questions and questions,"
He said with a sigh,
"One should not question a King!"
To which Sun replied, "Why?"

Well, the next thing he knew,
Sun was off to the East,
Toward the Mulberry Bridge,
To confront that Troll Beast.

And traveling with him,
In the back of the wagon,
Was a large stack of books,
And Yester, the dragon.

They went without weapons,
No sword, shield or lance,
But Sun did wear his armor;
Including the pants!

They'd try to use reason,
But one never knew,
One could not predict,
What a Bridge Troll might do!

Through Pachyderm Forest,
Where tiny elephants play,
Down the cobblestone path,
That guided their way;

They passed through the land
Where Tree Gnomes reside,
And even spotted a few,
Before they managed to hide.

The stone road was bumpy,
The ride was quite rough,
And it made Yester's reading,
Exceedingly tough.

And while Sun drove the wagon,
Thinking what he might do,
Yester read from a book,
Titled: "Bridge Trolls ----- and You!"

"It says here on page twelve,"
The dragon declared,
"That despite their great size,
They're quite easily scared."

"Of sudden loud noises
To be rather exact,
And this book is quite rare,
So it's a little known fact."

"A Troll is a creature,
I've not actually seen,
But there's a picture in here,
It's on page seventeen."

"There's a picture?" asked Sun,
"I'd best have a look."
So he turned in the wagon,
And stared at the book.

"Do you think that it's true?"
The boy asked his old friend,
"Because Mulberry Bridge,
Is around the next bend!"

Before Yester could answer,
It came into sight,
Great Mulberry Bridge,
Over the River of Light.

And there on the bridge,
Stood the mighty Bridge Troll,
His left hand extended,
To collect the bridge toll.

He seemed so much bigger,
And he looked awfully mean,
Not at all like the Troll
On page seventeen!

His ears, long and pointed,
His skin, orange and brown,
And his arms were so long,
That they just touched the ground.

"Let's have your money,"
The Bridge Troll began,
"If you want to cross HERE,
Put it THERE in my hand!"

Now at the foot of the bridge,
Sun had halted the wagon,
And while he climbed down,
Out sprang Yester, the dragon.

Gazing up at the Troll,
He felt tiny and small,
But then Sun shouted out,
"Why should we pay you at all?"

"I've no idea why,"
The Troll said with a grin,
"That's just how it is,
As it always has been."

"Trolls build the bridges,
Then collect a bridge toll!
That's just what you do
When you're a Bridge Troll!"

"So, if you're not going to pay,
You'd best know how to fight,
Or you're going to end up,
In the River of Light."

Then as the great Troll,
Moved to the attack,
The air all around them,
Turned suddenly black.

And along with the darkness,
Came a thunderous sound,
That shook the great bridge,
From the top to the ground.

The land was a-tremble,
The sky full of smoke,
The air was so thick,
That a person could choke.

And it so frightened the Troll,
That he started to quiver,
And trembling and shaking,
He jumped into the river.

Then as the air cleared,
Sun had a good laugh,
Calling down to the Troll,
"Are you taking a bath?"

But the Troll was confused,
He could not answer just now,
He had to find out,
What had happened, somehow.

So he waded to shore,
His eyes searching around,
Trying to determine,
The source of that sound.

And seeing the dragon,
He suddenly froze,
As he noticed the smoke,
Wafting up from its nose.

Could that be a dragon?
He'd not seen one before;
And what if it were?
Could it make such a roar?

"What was that noise?"
The Troll asked with surprise,
"It couldn't have come,
From something THAT SIZE!"

"Not only can, but it did!"
Yester said with a grin,
"And you'd better behave,
Lest I do it again."

"You can do that again?
Oh, no," cried the Troll,
Then softly he asked,
"But, how did you know?"

So Sun held up the book,
And said, "Here's how he knew!
It's right here in this book,
It's called 'Bridge Trolls ----- and You'!"

For the first time in his life,
The mighty Bridge Troll,
Found himself in a spot,
That he couldn't control.

Because of that book,
He could no longer stand,
And collect those bridge tolls,
In his large out-stretched hand.

"So what happens now?"
He asked Yester and Sun,
"I guess it's up to you,
As it seems you have won."

"I do have an idea,"
Sun said with a smile,
So they all sat on the bridge,
And they talked for awhile.

As it turned out, you see,
That Troll wasn't so bad,
And he had a real name,
It was Herkimer Thadd.

Collecting bridge tolls,
Was all that Herkimer knew,
And if he couldn't do that,
Well, then what would he do?

Sun had the answer,
A deal could be made,
If they could agree,
On one simple trade.

In exchange for a bridge,
With no toll and no guard,
They'd give Herkimer Thadd,
A King's Library Card!

The great Troll liked this,
And he quickly agreed,
"Just imagine," he said,
"All the books I could read!"

"No more collecting those tolls?
No more having to fight?
No more tossing folks into
The River of Light?"

"No more standing up there,
Hot and bored all the time?
Let's put this in writing!
Tell me, where do I sign?"

That being settled,
Sun climbed into the wagon,
With Herkimer Thadd,
And Yester the dragon.

And off they all went,
To meet with the King,
To explain to him how
They'd resolved this whole thing.

King Week was quite pleased,
And he said to young Sun,
"I will dub you a knight,
For what you have done!"

"No thank you," said Sun.
"That job's not for me.
A librarian, Sire,
Is what I wish to be!"

"I hate all this armor,
And I don't like to smite,
So, you'd have to admit,
I'd make one lousy knight!"

The King was so shocked,
He didn't know what to say,
It just wasn't suppose,
To happen this way.

But he thought of it more,
And it came to him then,
Things don't HAVE to remain,
As they always have been.

When we no longer know,
Why we do what we do,
Then perhaps it is time,
To do something new!

And to remember this always,
The King then proclaimed,
That the first day of the week,
Would now be renamed.

"In honor of Sun,"
He went on to say,
"Instead of Day 1,
We'll call it Sunday!"

Hear ye! Hear ye!
Be it ever known:
This King's Library Card,
When presented and shown,
Entitles: *Herkimer Thadd*
To come and peruse,
And borrow and read,
Any book he may choose.